TAKE TEN YEARS

1980s

Library of Congress Cataloging-in-Publication Data

Twist, Clint.
  1980s / Clint Twist.
       p.   cm. — (Take ten years)
  Includes index.
  Summary: Examines the top news stories of the 1980s, including war in Iran and Iraq, AIDS, and the opening of the Berlin Wall.
  ISBN 0–8114–3081–2
  1. History, Modern—1945—Juvenile literature.   [1. History, Modern—1945–]   I. Title.   II. Series
  D848.T93   1994   92–40348
  909′.82—dc20   CIP
                                               AC

Typeset by Multifacit Graphics, Keyport, NJ
Printed in Spain by GRAFO, S.A., Bilbao
Bound in the United States by Lake Book, Melrose Park, IL
1 2 3 4 5 6 7 8 9 0 LB 99 98 97 96 95 94

Acknowledgments

Maps — Jillian Luff, Bitmap Graphics
Design — Neil Sayer
Editor — Caroline Sheldrick

For permission to reproduce copyright material the author and publishers gratefully acknowledge the following:

Cover photographs — (left) NASA; (from top) © Chip Hires/Gamma-Liason, AP/Wide World Photos, National Archives, AP/Wide World Photos

Page 4 — (from top) UPI/Bettmann, Topham, S. Salgado/Magnum, Steve Rapport/Retna; page 5 (from top) — Topham, G. Pinkhassov/Magnum Photos, Alex Webb/Magnum, Associated Press/Topham, Associated Press/Topham; page 8 — Peter Marlow/Magnum; page 9 — (left and right) Topham; page 10 — (center top) Allsport, (center) Associated Press/Topham, (center bottom) Topham, (bottom right) David McGough/Retna; page 11 — Topham; page 12 — The Hulton Picture Company; page 13 — NASA/Science Photo Library; page 14 — (top) Topham, (bottom) Barnaby's Picture Library; page 15 — Topham; page 16 — AP/Wide World Photos; page 17 — (left) Associated Press/Topham, (right) Topham; page 18 — AP/Wide World Photos; page 19 — Lawrence Livermore National Laboratory/Science Photo Library; page 20 — Abbas/Magnum Photos; page 21 — (top) Frank Micelotta/Retna, (bottom) Bekes of Cowes (UK); page 22 — UPI/Bettmann; page 23 — (top) Topham, (bottom) Associated Press/Topham; page 24 — (left, right) Associated Press/Topham; page 25 — Steve Rapport/Retna; page 26 — (top) Associated Press/Topham, (bottom) Topham; page 27 — (left) UPI/Bettmann, (right) David Hurn/Magnum Photos; page 28 — Novosti/Science Photo Library; page 29 — (top) Associated Press/Topham, (bottom) Adrian Morgan Ecoscene; page 30 — (top) Paul Grundy 1985/Robert Harding Picture Library, (bottom left) Popperfoto, (bottom right) Barnaby's Picture Library; page 31 — Topham; page 32 — (left and right) Associated Press/Topham; page 33 — (left) Associated Press/Topham, (right) Popperfoto; page 34 — Associated Press/Topham; page 35 — (center) AP/Wide World Photos, (left) Topham; page 36 — Associated Press/Topham; page 37 — (top) Frank Spooner Pictures/Gamma, (bottom) Fred Mayer/Magnum Photos; page 38 — Associated Press/Topham; page 39 — (top and bottom) Associated Press/Topham; page 40 — (left) Topham, (right) Gideon Mendel/Magnum Photos; page 41 — (top) Associated Press/Topham, (bottom) Gilles Peress/Magnum Photos; page 42 — (left) Alex Webb/Magnum, (right) Topham; page 43 — (top left) NASA, (bottom and right) Associated Press/Topham; page 44 — (1) Andrew McClenaghan/Science Photo Library, (2) Martin Bond/Science Photo Library, (3) Ray Ellis/Science Photo Library, (4) Philippe Plailly/Science Photo Library, (5) NASA; page 45 — (1) Trippett/Sipa-Press/Rex Features, (2) and (3) Aviation Picture Library, (4) Harvey Pincis/Science Photo Library

1980s

CLINT TWIST

**RAINTREE
STECK-VAUGHN**
P U B L I S H E R S
The Steck-Vaughn Company

Austin, Texas

Contents

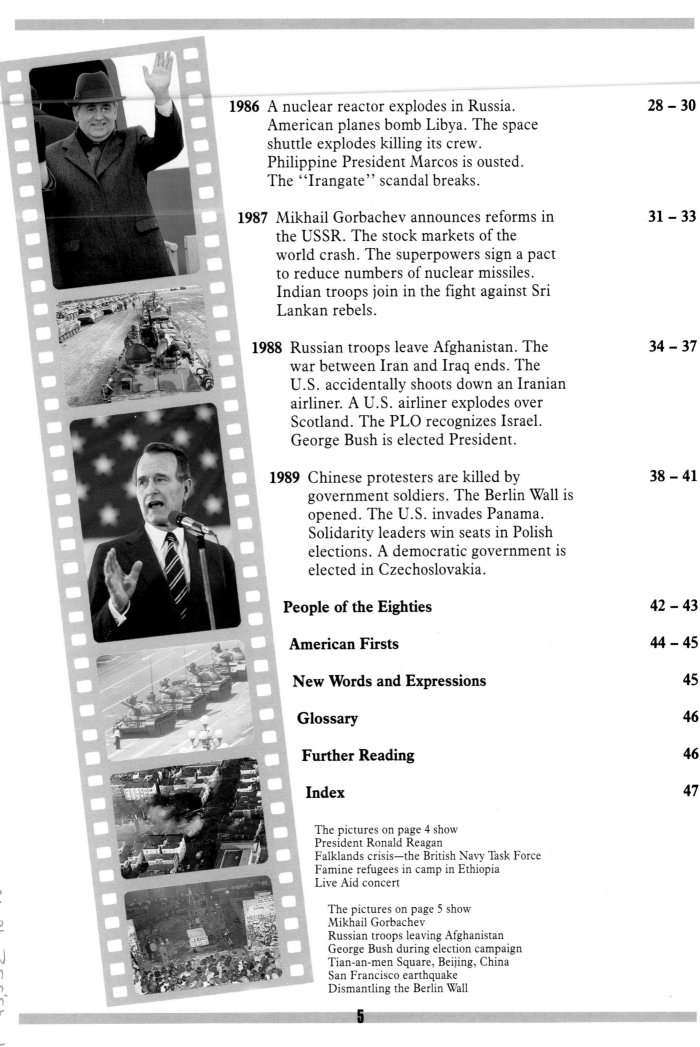

The pictures on page 4 show
President Ronald Reagan
Falklands crisis—the British Navy Task Force
Famine refugees in camp in Ethiopia
Live Aid concert

The pictures on page 5 show
Mikhail Gorbachev
Russian troops leaving Afghanistan
George Bush during election campaign
Tian-an-men Square, Beijing, China
San Francisco earthquake
Dismantling the Berlin Wall

Introduction

The Eighties was a decade of political violence, much as the Seventies had been. Three major conflicts dragged on for nearly the whole ten years. Iran and Iraq fought each other to a standstill. Thousands died, but in the end, neither side could claim a victory. In Afghanistan, the mujahaddin fought a long and lonely war against the Russian invaders. On the shores of the Mediterranean, Lebanon was torn apart by internal strife and foreign invasion. Smaller wars, such as the one fought over the Falkland Islands, also made the headlines. There was a series of assassination attempts, some of them fatal. All over the world, there was pressure for change.

At the beginning of the Eighties, the main new power was militant Islam. In Tehran, the Ayatollah Khomeini preached Islamic fundamentalism, imposing strict traditional values on Iranian society. His teachings appealed to poor people in many Muslim countries.

Russia was still a superpower, but began to feel the need for political change. The Afghan war was unpopular, and the shops were empty of the things people wanted to buy. There was an urgent need for reform. A strong leader emerged. Mikhail Gorbachev announced new policies of *glasnost* (openness) and *perestroika* (reconstruction).

By the late Eighties, there was similar unrest throughout the Communist countries of Eastern Europe. The leader of this movement was the Polish trade union, Solidarity. For most of the Eighties, Solidarity was a lone voice calling for democracy. However, with East Germany's "October Revolution" of 1989, the reunification of East and West Germany was in sight. And by the end of the decade, a wave of reform was sweeping across Eastern Europe.

Democracy also spread to other parts of the globe. In China, it flourished very briefly, before being crushed by the authorities. In the Philippines, a dictator was overthrown, and a democratic government was formed.

In the United States, the Eighties was generally a decade of prosperity, despite a disastrous stock market crash. Yet it was also a time of concern, both for the suffering of other people and for the future of the planet as a whole.

YEARS	WORLD AFFAIRS
1980	U.S. hostage rescue attempt fails in Iran. British rescue hostages in Iranian embassy. Robert Mugabe becomes Zimbabwe's prime minister.
1981	American hostages in Iran released. Martial law declared in Poland. Belize gains independence from Britain.
1982	PLO evicted from Lebanon by Israelis. Massacre of Palestinian refugees Socialists win power in Spain. Solidarity trade union banned in Poland.
1983	Syrians evict PLO from Lebanon. OPEC cuts world price of oil.
1984	Famine in Ethiopia
1985	Mikhail Gorbachev comes to power in USSR. Anglo-Irish Agreement signed. AIDS declared an epidemic.
1986	President Marcos of Philippines is ousted. "Irangate" scandal in America
1987	Gorbachev announces reforms in USSR. Fiji gains independence.
1988	Independence gained for Namibia. PLO recognizes state of Israel.
1989	Berlin Wall opened. Solidarity wins elections in Poland. Hungary opens its border with Austria.

WARS & CIVIL DISORDER	PEOPLE	EVENTS
War between Iran and Iraq	Lech Walesa leads Polish Solidarity. Ronald Reagan becomes President. Actor Peter Sellers dies. Ex-Beatle John Lennon shot dead.	Volcano erupts in Washington State. U.S. boycotts Olympic Games in Moscow.
Coup attempt in Spain fails. U.S. Embassy in San Salvador attacked.	Assassination of President Sadat of Egypt François Mitterrand elected president of France. President Reagan shot and wounded.	Doctors identify new disease, AIDS. Space shuttle launched in U.S. First woman, Sandra Day O'Connor, appointed to Supreme Court.
War in Falkland Islands Sandinista regime suspends civil rights in Nicaragua.	Leonid Brezhnev of USSR dies. "Moonie" leader guilty of income tax evasion.	European Court bans corporal punishment in schools. W. Germany gets left-wing chancellor. Disney World opens EPCOT.
Islamic fundamentalists bomb troops in Beirut. U.S. invades Grenada.	Margaret Thatcher reelected in Britain. Benigno Aquino murdered in Philippines. Lech Walesa wins Nobel Peace Prize.	Russia shoots down Korean airliner. U.S. announces "Star Wars" defense system. Australia wins America's Cup.
	Indira Gandhi assassinated. Polish priest killed for supporting Solidarity. Ronald Reagan reelected President.	Russians boycott Olympic Games. Doctors identify AIDS virus. Chemical factory disaster in India
PLO hijacks Italian cruise ship. Soccer riot kills 41 fans in Belgium.	Orson Welles, actor and filmmaker, dies. French secret agents jailed for attack on Greenpeace ship.	Live Aid concerts for Ethiopia Earthquake in Mexico kills thousands. Wreck of *Titanic* found on seabed.
U.S. planes bomb Libya.	Olaf Palme, Swedish prime minister, assassinated. Sculptor Henry Moore dies.	Chernobyl nuclear reactor disaster U.S. space shuttle explodes on takeoff. Chemicals pollute Rhine.
Indian and Sri Lankan troops fight Tamils. Afghan rebels fight Russians.	Andy Warhol, artist, dies. German teenager flies alone to Moscow.	Stock markets of the world crash. Over $32 million paid for a Van Gogh. U.S. and USSR sign arms treaty.
Russian troops leave Afghanistan. Iran and Iraq end their war.	President Reagan broadcasts to Russia. George Bush elected President. Benazir Bhutto elected in Pakistan.	U.S. ship shoots down Iranian airliner. U.S. airliner explodes over Scotland. Australian bicentennial celebrations North Sea gas rig explodes.
Protesters massacred in China. Democracy demonstrations in East Germany and Georgia, USSR Revolution in Romania U.S. invades Panama.	ANC's Walter Sisulu freed from jail. President Ceausescu of Romania executed. Vaclav Havel, playwright, elected Czech president.	San Francisco hit by earthquake. Oil spill in Alaska Supreme Court says flag burning constitutional.

1980

HOSTAGE RESCUE BIDS

U.S. TROOPS FAIL TO RESCUE HOSTAGES

April 25, Tehran, Iran A secret force of American commandos has failed in its attempt to rescue a group of U.S. hostages. Nearly 100 hostages are being held in the occupied U.S. Embassy here in Iran. They were taken hostage in the embassy in November last year. The rescue mission by the U.S. Delta Force ended in disaster when two aircraft collided and burst into flames. They were refueling in the Iranian desert.

Helicopters carrying American troops had taken off from an aircraft carrier sailing in the Persian Gulf. They were still some 180 miles (300 km) from their target when disaster struck. Eight servicemen died in the accident. The mission was immediately called off.

FAILURE A BLOW TO CARTER

April 26, Washington President Carter has taken the blame for the failure of the Iran rescue mission. This may affect his chances of being reelected later this year. Abroad, the desert disaster has spoiled America's all-powerful image. In Iran, the Ayatollah Khomeini will be pleased that America, which he calls "the Great Satan," has lost prestige.

Police officers keep the public at a safe distance as rescuers retake the Iranian Embassy. The assault ends a six-day siege of the embassy, held by Iranian terrorists.

LONDON EMBASSY HOSTAGES RESCUED

May 5, London A team from the British Special Air Service (SAS) today had a dramatic shoot-out with armed terrorists. Six days ago, the Iranian Embassy in London was seized by anti-Khomeini terrorists. They demanded that political prisoners in Iran be released. The people inside the embassy, diplomats and visitors alike, were taken hostage.

This afternoon, black-clad figures slid down the roof and crashed through the windows. For a few minutes the crackle of automatic gunfire could be heard, and then it was all over. The hostages were free, and all but one of the terrorists were dead.

WAR BETWEEN IRAN AND IRAQ

Sept. 25, Abadan, Iran Iraqi tanks yesterday led an attack on Iran. The Iraqi Army crossed the border in several places and began advancing into Iranian territory. One of the first places to be attacked was the world's largest oil refinery at Abadan.

Relations between the two Arab countries have been bad for some time. One of the main causes of dispute is the Sha'at al Arab waterway, which forms part of the border between them. The Iraqi leader, Saddam Hussein, says only the Iraqis can use this vital outlet to the sea.

FREE TRADE UNION IN POLAND

Sept. 22, Gdansk, Poland Polish workers have won the right to form an independent trade union. The government gave in to workers' demands after months of strikes. The new trade union is called Solidarity. Its leader is Lech Walesa, an electrician at the Gdansk shipyards. (Gdansk was once known as Danzig.) Solidarity is the first independent trade union ever to be permitted in a Communist country.

Ronald Reagan and his wife Nancy.

MARXIST PRIME MINISTER FOR ZIMBABWE

March 4, Harare, Zimbabwe Robert Mugabe has been elected prime minister of newly independent Zimbabwe. He is the first black leader of this African country (which was formerly called Rhodesia, and ruled by the white minority). Mugabe is a Marxist and a believer in black majority rule. However, he is expected to make concessions to the rich whites who control most of Zimbabwe's industry and agriculture.

The statue of Cecil Rhodes, founder of Rhodesia, is pulled down by jubilant Zimbabweans.

CARTER LOSES ELECTION

Nov. 4, Washington The Republican candidate, Ronald Reagan, has been elected the next U.S. President. The new Vice-President is to be George Bush. Reagan defeated Jimmy Carter by a large majority. Carter lost popularity after the failure of the hostage rescue attempt in April.

Both newcomers have been in politics for some time. Reagan has served as governor of California, and Bush was formerly head of the CIA. Before entering politics, Reagan was a film actor.

NEWS IN BRIEF . . .

SMALLPOX A DISEASE OF THE PAST

May 8, Geneva, Switzerland The World Health Organization has today announced that smallpox has been wiped out. Their worldwide vaccination campaign has been a success. For centuries this infectious disease has killed most of its victims, and left survivors with pockmarked faces. The last reported case was in Somalia in the late 1970s. Scientists now believe that the threat of smallpox has gone forever.

Daley Thompson of the United Kingdom at the Moscow Olympics.

VOLCANO ERUPTS IN WASHINGTON

May 19, state of Washington A dormant volcano south of Seattle, has erupted, killing at least eight people. After rumbling for weeks, Mount St. Helens exploded today, showering ash over a wide area. In places the ash fall is more than 33 feet (10 m) deep. Houses and cars have been buried. Floods and mud slides caused by the eruption have also caused much damage.

MAN OF 1,000 FACES DIES

July 24, Switzerland The British actor Peter Sellers has died. Sellers was one of the world's best-loved comedy actors, and was a master of disguise. He first became well known doing the voices of several weird characters in a British radio comedy. In some of his films he also played several different roles. Probably his most famous character was the accident-prone French detective Inspector Clouseau, in the *Pink Panther* films.

U.S. BOYCOTTS MOSCOW OLYMPICS

Aug. 3, Moscow The 22nd Olympic Games ended today. There have been no competitors from our country, West Germany, or Kenya. Some individual athletes from other countries also refused to attend the games. These countries and individuals boycotted the Olympics in protest of the Russian invasion of Afghanistan, which began late last year.

PERSONAL STEREO SUCCESS

Dec. 31, Tokyo, Japan The most popular accessory in the world this year is the "Walkman" personal stereo system produced by the huge Sony company. "Walkman" is a tiny cassette player, equipped with a pair of lightweight headphones. Easily carried on a belt, "Walkman" enables active people to enjoy music while they walk, jog, or bicycle.

JOHN LENNON SHOT

Dec. 8, New York Ex-Beatle John Lennon has been shot dead in a New York street. Lennon, aged 40, was returning home with his wife, Yoko Ono, when a gunman opened fire at close range. Police have arrested the killer, who claims to be one of John Lennon's greatest fans.

1981

LEADERS ARE GUNMEN'S TARGETS

POPE WOUNDED IN ASSASSINATION ATTEMPT

May 13, Vatican City, Italy Pope John Paul II has been seriously wounded by a lone gunman. The pope was riding in an open-topped vehicle when shots rang out. He was rushed to a hospital, where surgeons removed four bullets. Doctors say that the pope is expected to make a full recovery.

Immediately after the shooting, police arrested Mehmet Agca, a 23-year-old Armenian. Agca is wanted by the Turkish police for the murder of a leading Turkish journalist. He claims he shot the pope as a protest against the warlike behavior of the two superpowers. Many people think there was another motive, however. They suspect that Agca may have been hired by an Eastern European country. Communist governments are known to be angry at the pope's support for the Polish Solidarity trade union movement.

PRESIDENT REAGAN SHOT

March 30, Washington A man today shot and wounded President Reagan and three other people. The shots were fired as the President left a hotel in town. Secret Service agents immediately overpowered the attacker and handed him over to police. The President was taken to a hospital where a bullet was removed from near his heart. Hospital spokespersons say that the President is now out of danger. He is in good spirits, and is said to be making jokes with his doctors.

SADAT OF EGYPT ASSASSINATED

Oct. 6, Cairo, Egypt President Anwar Sadat has been shot dead during a military parade. The assassins were dressed in army uniforms, and so far no one knows who they were.

President Sadat won the Nobel Peace Prize for making peace with Israel. But in doing so, he made many enemies in the Arab world. Many people wanted him dead. Most likely, he was killed by members of the Muslim Brotherhood, an Islamic fundamentalist organization. The Egyptian vice-president, Hosni Mubarak, takes over as head of state until elections can be held.

A security man shouts instructions after the assassination of President Sadat.

TEHRAN HOSTAGES RELEASED

Jan. 21, Tehran, Iran The American Embassy hostages have been released. Last night, they were flown to Algeria, from where they will be returned to the United States. The hostages spent a total of 444 days in captivity. They were released on the day after President Reagan's inauguration. Ayatollah Khomeini meant this as a final snub to ex-President Carter, who failed to rescue the hostages. Friends and relatives are celebrating.

NEW PRIME MINISTER FOR POLAND

Feb. 9, Warsaw, Poland There are still strikes and unrest in Poland, even though workers have the Solidarity trade union to back them. The Communist leaders have appointed General Wojciech Jaruzelski as prime minister. Jaruzelski is a moderate, and may have been chosen because Solidarity might agree to negotiate with him. However, he is also a soldier. The authorities may be planning military conflict with the union.

ATTEMPTED COUP IN SPAIN

Feb. 24, Madrid, Spain Rebel members of the Civil Guard yesterday took over the Spanish parliament building. They fired automatic weapons, and took about 350 members hostage. At first, some army units seemed to be supporting the rebels. However, they returned to their barracks after a television broadcast by King Juan Carlos. Shortly afterward, the Civil Guards surrendered to the authorities. They are believed to be right-wing extremists who want an end to parliamentary government.

WOMAN APPOINTED TO SUPREME COURT

July 7, Washington President Reagan today named Sandra Day O'Connor an associate justice of the U.S. Supreme Court. She is the first woman to be appointed to the Court. Born in Texas, O'Connor received her law degree from Stanford University. She conducted a private law practice in Phoenix, Arizona, and became an assistant attorney general there. She served as a state senator, and later as a county trial court judge. In 1979 she became a judge on the Arizona Court of Appeals.

GISCARD OUT—MITTERRAND IN

May 10, Paris, France The Socialist politician François Mitterrand has been elected president of France. He defeated Giscard d'Estaing by a decisive majority. Mitterrand is the first Socialist to lead France for more than 20 years. Although he will follow left-wing policies at home, he is a firm supporter of the NATO alliance.

AIR TRAFFIC CONTROLLERS FIRED

Aug. 6, Washington Federal air traffic controllers have been on strike for three days. They have ignored a judge's back-to-work order. The strike has grounded more than 7,000 airline flights a day. Now President Reagan has fired all 12,000 strikers. The controllers union had been hoping that the government would come to some agreement with the strikers on issues such as higher pay, fewer hours, and a better retirement plan. The union claimed the strike would cause serious problems at airport control towers. But an official of the Federal Aviation Administration claims the controllers' work is being done by other trained professionals.

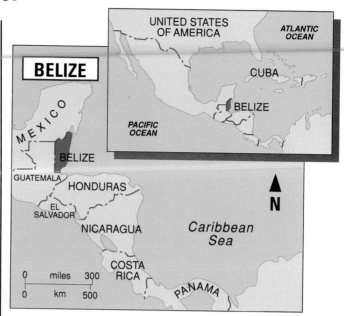

INDEPENDENCE FOR BELIZE

Sept. 20, Belize City, Belize Belize in Central America has become independent. It was formerly British Honduras. Months of difficult negotiations were held with Honduras and Guatemala. These neighboring countries have threatened to invade. As a result, British troops will be staying on in order to protect Belize's borders.

MARTIAL LAW IN POLAND

Dec. 14, Warsaw, Poland In a surprise move, General Jaruzelski yesterday imposed martial law to crush the Solidarity movement. Tanks have been used to break up demonstrations and deter protesting crowds. Several workers have been killed. Thousands of Solidarity members, includng leader Lech Walesa, have been arrested. The Catholic Church in Poland continues to support Solidarity.

FIRST SPACE SHUTTLE LAUNCH

April 11, Florida The first U.S. space shuttle, *Columbia*, was today launched like a rocket into orbit. The shuttle belongs to a new generation of reusable spacecraft. After its three-day space mission, *Columbia* will reenter the earth's atmosphere, and land like an airplane. The astronauts appeared live on television.

NEWS IN BRIEF . . .

PRINCE CHARLES MARRIES

July 29, London Charles, Britain's Prince of Wales, today married Lady Diana Spencer. Our own First Lady, Nancy Reagan, was among the guests at St. Paul's Cathedral. An estimated world-wide audience of 700 million watched the ceremony via TV. The royal romance has been news for months in the popular press. The wedding has started rumors that Charles's mother, Queen Elizabeth, may abdicate. If she does, Charles will become king of England.

BOB MARLEY DIES

May 11, Florida The Jamaican reggae musician Bob Marley has died in a hospital here of cancer. Marley, aged 36, was the king of reggae, with its slow, insistent beat. He was popular with both black and white audiences and had a worldwide following. Recently, Marley had become involved in Jamaican politics. He worked for peace and unity between rival political parties on that island.

U.S. EMBASSY ATTACKED

March 25, El Salvador The U.S. Embassy in San Salvador, El Salvador's capital city, was badly damaged by gunfire today. This nation is ruled by a junta government under President José Duarte. This government is supported by the United States. Responsibility for today's attack is claimed by leftist guerrillas who want to stop American military and economic aid to the government. President Reagan has recently increased this aid.

NEW IMMUNE DEFICIENCY DISEASE

Dec. 30, Los Angeles Doctors here and in New York have identified a new killer disease. Victims lose weight rapidly and then die from infection. The disease affects the human immune system and its ability to fight illnesses. Over 150 cases have been reported this year, nearly all of them among male homosexuals.

CHRISTY BROWN DIES

Sept. 7, Dublin The Irish writer and artist Christy Brown has died at the age of 48. Brown was a remarkable character. He was almost completely paralyzed from birth, and could only move his left foot. Typing just with the toes of one foot, he wrote a best-selling autobiography, *Down All Our Days*.

"NO CRUISE" DEMONSTRATION

Oct. 24, London Over 150,000 peace protesters crowded into London's Hyde Park today. They oppose the deployment of American cruise missiles in Britain. Cruise missiles are the newest long-range American nuclear weapons. With a range of about 621 miles (1,000 km) they fly at low level like tiny aircraft and are very hard to detect. The protesters say that having cruise missiles makes the country a likelier target for attack.

1982

WAR OVER FALKLAND ISLANDS

FALKLAND ISLANDS INVADED

April 2, Port Stanley, Falkland Islands Argentinian troops today invaded these remote British islands in the South Atlantic. About 100 British soldiers were taken prisoner in a daring night attack. The invasion has taken the British government completely by surprise. For many years, Argentina has said it owns the Falkland Islands, which it calls Islas Malvinas. However, there were no signs that Argentina was about to invade.

British Prime Minister Margaret Thatcher announced that the government will send a task force of men and ships to retake the Falkland Islands. When the task force is ready, it will sail 7,765 miles (12,500 km) to the South Atlantic.

In Buenos Aires, the Argentinian capital, there are celebrations. Thousands turned out to cheer General Galtieri, the country's military leader, when he announced that Las Malvinas had been recaptured.

HMS *Fearless* leaves for the Falkland Islands as part of the British task force.

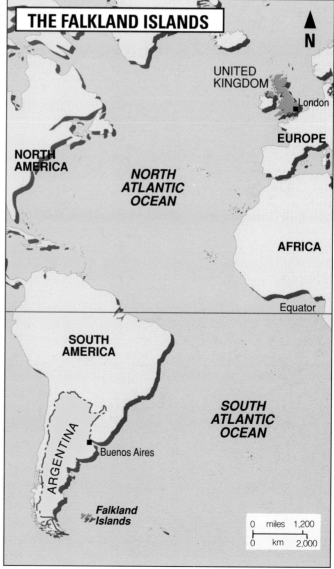

THE FALKLAND ISLANDS

BRITISH AND ARGENTINIAN WARSHIPS SUNK

May 4, Buenos Aires A British warship HMS *Sheffield* was today destroyed. Twenty men died, and many more were wounded. It was hit by an Exocet missile fired from an Argentinian aircraft. The missile attack seems to be in revenge for the sinking of the Argentinian warship *General Belgrano* two days ago. The *General Belgrano* was the only Argentinian warship at sea. It posed a threat to the British task force now on its way to the Falkland Islands. It was sunk by a British submarine, and over 400 Argentinians drowned.

HMS *Sheffield* (left) shortly before sinking.

CIVIL RIGHTS SUSPENDED IN NICARAGUA

March 25, Managua, Nicaragua Daniel Ortega is head of the government of Nicaragua—the Sandinista regime. For 10 days there has been a state of emergency here after rioting and guerrilla activity against Ortega's government. Today he announced that for 30 days all civil rights will be suspended, including the right to freedom of expression. Ortega said he is taking this step because he blames the U.S. for the attacks. He says the U.S. has "plans of aggression against our country." He claims the U.S. plans to use anti-Sandinista exiles to overthrow the Sandinista regime. The U.S. denies this. The Sandinistas have been in power since 1979. That year, after a long guerrilla war, they overthrew a corrupt and cruel government led by the Somoza family. The original leader, Anastasio Somoza, was supported by the U.S. Opposing the Somoza government were nationalist forces led by Augusto Sandino. The present Nicaraguan regime is named for that leader.

PLANE HITS POTOMAC BRIDGE

Jan. 13, Washington During a snowstorm today, a jet crashed into a bridge and sank into the Potomac River, killing 78 people. The crash caused a huge traffic jam. Emergency vehicles had to drive on sidewalks to reach the scene. Horrified commuters watched as passengers struggled and sank into the icy waters.

ARGENTINIAN FORCES SURRENDER

June 14, Port Stanley The last Argentinian forces in the Falklands surrendered today. They were completely surrounded in the capital, Port Stanley. This final British success follows that of two weeks ago, when paratroops recaptured the Goose Green airfield. In both cases, large numbers of Argentinian soldiers surrendered to smaller and better-equipped British forces. Two-and-a-half months after the Argentinian invasion, the Falkland Islands are once again under British rule.

ISRAEL EVICTS THE PLO

Aug. 31, Beirut, Lebanon The Israeli Army has forced the Palestine Liberation Organization (PLO) out of Lebanon. For years, the PLO has used Lebanon as a base for attacks on Israel. Today, PLO leader Yasser Arafat left Beirut to join his 7,000 fighters in exile. Most of them have gone to sympathetic Arab countries such as Syria, Iraq, and Algeria.

Israel invaded Lebanon at the beginning of June. Very soon, the PLO was under siege in its Beirut headquarters. There was also fierce fighting around the PLO strongholds in Sidon and Tyre. Syrian forces were in ferocious tank clashes with Israelis on the road to Damascus. More than 60 Syrian aircraft were shot down. Most of the Lebanese Muslim population, which includes many Palestinian refugees, support the PLO. Christian inhabitants, and members of a Syrian sect called Druse, are against them.

MASSACRES IN LEBANON

Sept. 17, Beirut There has been bloodshed following the PLO's departure from Beirut. Today, Christian militia began murdering the Palestinian refugees in camps at Sabra and Chatila. Already, hundreds of men, women, and children are reported dead. Lebanon's Christian prime minister was killed earlier this week, and the massacre was a revenge attack. Israeli troops have done nothing to prevent the killings. Some Palestinians say the Israelis helped the Christian militia.

A damaged street in Beirut.

NEW CHANCELLOR FOR WEST GERMANY

Oct. 1, Bonn, West Germany Helmut Schmidt, the leader of the left-wing Social Democrat party, has been fired as chancellor of West Germany. The Bonn parliament today voted to replace him with Helmut Kohl, the leader of the right-wing Christian Democrat party. Members of parliament hope that Christian Democrat policies will reduce public spending and cut unemployment.

SOLIDARITY BANNED

Oct. 8, Warsaw, Poland Solidarity, the independent trade union, has been banned by Poland's Communist government. Spokesmen for the union, which is now illegal, said that they would continue to operate in secret. They urged supporters not to become involved in mass demonstrations that would provoke violence.

SOCIALIST VICTORY IN SPAIN

Oct. 28, Madrid, Spain The Socialist party has won a landslide victory in the Spanish elections. The moderate center parties appear to have collapsed completely. The new parliament will be sharply divided between a left-wing majority, and a right-wing minority. The new prime minister will be Felipe Gonzalez. Aged just 40, he will become Europe's youngest national leader.

ANDROPOV REPLACES BREZHNEV

Nov. 10, Moscow President Leonid Brezhnev has died of a heart attack, aged 75. The new Russian leader will be Yuri Andropov, who was formerly head of the KGB, the Russian secret police. Although Andropov has been tough with his rivals, he is expected to be more liberal in some policies. Brezhnev held very old-fashioned views, and he failed to reform the Russian economy so that it could compete with the West.

Yuri Andropov, the new Russian leader.

NEWS IN BRIEF . . .

ANTI-NUKE PROTEST

June 12, New York About 800,000 people demonstrated today in this city's streets and in Central Park. They were calling for an end to the increase of nuclear weapons. Leaders of the rally said this was the largest protest of this kind ever held in the U.S. Coretta Scott King, widow of Dr. Martin Luther King, Jr., was a speaker.

CORPORAL PUNISHMENT BANNED

Feb. 25, Strasbourg, France The European Court has banned the corporal punishment of children without their parents' consent. In effect, this means that schools will no longer be able to punish children by physical methods, such as the cane. Most parents support the court's decision, but some still believe that physical punishment is necessary in order to enforce discipline in schools.

MOONIE LEADER CONVICTED

May 18, Washington Sun Myung Moon, the leader of the Unification Church, has been found guilty of income tax evasion. Members of the church are often known as "Moonies." For months, Moon has been under investigation because of his extravagant life-style. He receives large donations from religious converts, most of them young people. Moonie groups have been accused of holding people against their will, brainwashing them into staying, and claiming them as converts.

ZIMBABWE'S LEADERS SPLIT

Feb. 17, Harare Since Zimbabwe became independent in 1980, the country's new prime minister, Robert Mugabe, has shared power with the veteran nationalist Joshua Nkomo. Today Mugabe dismissed Nkomo from his cabinet, along with two other ministers. The power struggle in Zimbabwe has ended.

SILICON CHIP REVOLUTION

Sept. 30, New York and London Another industrial revolution is in full swing in the industrialized nations. Microprocessors on silicon chips are now being used in workplaces, doing enormously varied work. Robots assembling cars, word processors in offices, information storage on discs, all rely on the "microchip."

E.T.–A LOVABLE ALIEN IS EVERYONE'S FAVORITE

Dec. 3, Hollywood The hit film of the year is *E.T.: The Extra-Terrestrial*, directed by Steven Spielberg. The film is about a being from another world who becomes stranded on earth. The alien is befriended by some children who help to organize a rescue mission. The film has the irresistible combination of a cute story, a cast of talented child actors, and some dazzling special effects. Children and adults alike are flocking to see *E.T.* The idea of intelligent, friendly beings in space has great appeal.

WALT DISNEY WORLD'S EPCOT ADDITION OPENS

Oct. 1, Orlando, Fla. Today a 260-acre companion park to Disney World opened. It is known as EPCOT (Experimental Prototype Community of Tomorrow) Center. Visitors will enter through a geodesic dome called "Spaceship Earth." The new park concentrates on science and technology. Its many futuristic exhibits include "Universe of Energy" and "Journey into Imagination." EPCOT was planned to provide amusement and education for adults as well as children.

1983

U.S. TO HAVE SPACE DEFENSE SYSTEM

March 23, Washington Today President Reagan announced that America is to develop a real-life "Star Wars" defense system. A system of satellites equipped with lasers and other advanced weapons would shoot down enemy missiles while they were still in flight. Reagan claimed that the Star Wars system would end the threat of a surprise nuclear attack. The term "Star Wars" comes from the name of a popular 1977 science-fiction film.

A technician at work in a "Star Wars" research laboratory.

BRITISH REELECT THATCHER

June 10, London The Conservative party has won the British general election, and Mrs. Margaret Thatcher has been reelected prime minister. Despite the growth in unemployment, the Conservatives won the election by a record majority.

One of the main reasons for this success is Margaret Thatcher herself. She is seen as a strong leader who will stand up for Britain.

POLITICAL ASSASSINATION AT AIRPORT

Aug. 21, Manila, Philippines A Filipino opposition leader has been assassinated minutes after he returned from exile. Benigno Aquino had just stepped off a plane from the United States when he was shot dead by a lone gunman. Aquino was a serious rival to President Ferdinand Marcos, and was going to run against him soon in an election.

RUSSIA SHOOTS DOWN KOREAN AIRLINER

Sept. 7, Moscow Russian jet fighters have shot down a South Korean airliner, killing all 269 passengers and crew. The incident happened a week ago, but the Russian authorities have only just admitted what happened. They claim that the airliner was on a spying mission for the United States, and was shot down over a secret military base. Our government has denied this, and says that the aircraft had accidentally strayed off course. South Korea has strong links with the United States, but it is unlikely that they would agree to use a civilian airliner for spying.

BEIRUT BOMBERS KILL HUNDREDS

Oct. 23, Beirut, Lebanon Islamic fundamentalists have killed more than 300 French and American soldiers in two bomb attacks. In both incidents, trucks full of explosives were driven into the military headquarters of peacekeeping forces. The drivers then set off the explosives, killing themselves along with their victims.

The more serious attack was at the U.S. Marine base, where over 250 Americans died. The other attack destroyed a multistory building and killed nearly 60 French paratroops. The marines and paratroops were part of the international peacekeeping force that moved into Beirut last year following the Israeli invasion. British and Italian troops are also stationed there to support the Lebanese Army.

Those responsible for the suicide attacks are believed to be Shiite Muslims who claim the Ayatollah Khomeini as their leader. They are opposed to the peacekeeping force because they believe that it supports the Christian militias. Beirut has become one of the most dangerous cities on earth. These attacks are not the only terrorist outrages this year. Earlier, a car bomb destroyed the U.S. Embassy.

U.S. INVADES GRENADA

Oct. 25, St. Georges, Grenada American combat troops have arrived on the Caribbean island of Grenada. In places, the local people fought the troops, and there have been some casualties.

The American soldiers were sent to restore democratic government to the island. Last week, Grenada's prime minister was murdered during what appears to be a leftist coup. In explaining his reasons for the invasion, President Reagan said it was to protect Americans living in Grenada. He said that the large numbers of Cuban workers on the island were really Communist soldiers.

PLO QUITS LEBANON AGAIN

Dec. 20, Tripoli, Lebanon Yasser Arafat and the PLO have been forced to leave Lebanon for the second time in two years. This time, they were forced out by the Syrian Army.

For the past three weeks, the Syrians and the PLO have fought for control of the Palestinian refugee camps. The better-equipped Syrians won. The PLO is now evacuating to Tunisia under the protection of the United Nations.

NEWS IN BRIEF . . .

MOST POPULAR TV SHOW

Feb. 28, New York A huge record television audience of 125 million Americans watched the final episode of *M.A.S.H.* tonight. *M.A.S.H.* is a long-running situation comedy set in a mobile army hospital during the Korean War. The scripts are extremely clever, and combine witty dialogue with antiwar satire.

OIL PRICE CUT

March 14, Washington How the times have changed. In contrast to the oil shortages and energy crisis of the 1970s, there is now a glut of oil and the price is coming down. For the first time in its history, the Organization of Petroleum Exporting Countries (OPEC) has said the price of oil will come down. Some economists believe that the cheapness of oil will cause a boom in the industrialized countries of the world.

HITLER DIARIES A FAKE!

May 6, Bonn, West Germany Two weeks ago, a German magazine published an amazing journalistic scoop: extracts from Adolf Hitler's personal diaries. Hitler was Germany's leader during World War II, and the diaries revealed some fascinating details. Many historians believed the diaries were genuine. Today, however, a panel of experts declared that the diaries were in fact extremely clever forgeries. Police are now looking for the forger who played an elaborate hoax on the press.

MADONNA'S CLOTHES SET TREND

Aug. 31, Detroit Madonna, a young female singer, may have started a new fashion trend that carries on where punk styles left off. On stage, Madonna has taken to wearing her underwear over the top of her other clothes. Audiences love it, and hundreds of girls are copying the Madonna look. She also uses energetic dance routines on stage. With a voice that is even better than her sense of style, Madonna looks set for success.

AMERICA'S CUP GOES TO AUSTRALIA

Sept. 23, Rhode Island For the first time in 132 years, America has lost the America's Cup, the world's most famous yacht racing trophy. Australia is the new holder of the cup, having beaten the U.S. by just one race. International yacht racing is extremely expensive. The victorious yacht, *Australia II*, is owned by a businessman.

The winning Australian crew.

PEACE PRIZE FOR SOLIDARITY LEADER

Dec. 10, Oslo, Norway Lech Walesa, leader of Poland's Solidarity trade union, has been awarded the Nobel Peace Prize. The Communist authorities have tried to put down the union, sometimes brutally. But Walesa has always kept up his policy of nonviolent opposition. By doing so, he has gained the support of the Catholic Church, which is against all forms of violence.

1984

WOMAN VICE-PRESIDENT POSSIBLE

July 12, St. Paul, Minn. Walter F. Mondale is expected to win the Democratic party nomination for President. Today he announced that he has chosen Geraldine Ferraro, U.S. representative of a district in Queens, New York City, to serve as his running mate. This will be the first time a woman has been chosen to run for Vice-President by a major party. Mondale, speaking from the steps of the Minnesota Capitol, said that he looked for the best Vice-President and "found her in Gerry Ferraro." In picking a woman, Mondale may be trying to put some new life into what many believe to be a hopeless challenge of the very popular Ronald Reagan.

Ferraro received her law degree from Fordham University. She became an assistant district attorney in Queens County in 1974. She was elected to Congress in 1978, 1980, and 1982. She is known as a strong liberal.

RUSSIANS BOYCOTT U.S. OLYMPICS

July 28, Los Angeles The Russians and most of their allies are boycotting the Los Angeles Olympic Games. Romania is the only country from the Soviet bloc taking part.

Four years ago, American athletes stayed away from the Moscow Olympics in protest over the Russian invasion of Afghanistan. This year, the Russians are claiming that they are worried about security at the games.

Sports fans all over the world wonder whether the Olympics will ever again be free of the shadow of international politics.

POLISH PRIEST MURDERED

Oct. 30, Warsaw, Poland A Catholic priest who was an active supporter of Solidarity has been murdered. The body of Father Jerzy Popieluszko was found in a reservoir earlier today. Father Popieluszko was a close friend of Lech Walesa, the Solidarity leader. He had spoken openly in his church against the government.

It is widely believed that the Polish secret police were behind the killing. If it is true, this was a bad mistake on the part of the authorities. The death of Father Popieluszko will unite Solidarity with the Polish Catholic Church in opposition to the Communist government and its policies. Solidarity continues to avoid violent demonstrations.

The Golden Temple of Amritsar in India, where Sikh extremists fought with Indian troops.

MRS. GANDHI ASSASSINATED

Oct. 31, New Delhi, India Indira Gandhi, prime minister of India, was assassinated by her own bodyguards today. She was on her way to a TV interview when two Sikh bodyguards shot her at close range. The new Indian prime minister is to be her second son, Rajiv Gandhi.

The assassination was a revenge attack. Mrs. Gandhi had allowed the Indian Army to evict militant Sikhs from the Golden Temple at Amritsar in June this year. Over 700 Sikhs died during four days of heavy fighting against tanks and artillery. Sikhs follow a different religion from the rest of India, which is mostly Hindu. Sikhs are traditionally warriors. Recently, Sikh extremists have been demanding their own independent Sikh state. Mrs. Gandhi and her government were firmly against these separatist ideas. Already there have been revenge attacks on Sikhs by Hindu mobs, killing, burning, and looting.

FAMINE IN EAST AFRICA

October, Addis Ababa, Ethiopia Seven million people here face starvation in one of the worst famines of modern times. Drought has again caused the crops to fail. The situation is made worse by a civil war in the north of the country.

When news of the famine reached the outside world, offers of help poured in from governments and from the general public. However, the authorities here seem to be inefficient and suspicious. So far, few of the relief shipments have reached the people of Ethiopia.

NEWS IN BRIEF . . .

REAGAN SIGNS CHINA ACCORDS

April 30, Beijing President Reagan has signed scientific and cultural agreements with China. He also OK'd a tax accord to improve business relations.

MYSTERY DISEASE EXPLAINED

April 23, Washington Doctors have isolated the virus that causes the killer disease referred to as AIDS (Acquired Immune Deficiency Syndrome).

AIDS was first reported in 1981 among male homosexuals. However, doctors now say that AIDS is spreading to other sections of society. Although they have found the virus, they admit that it may be many years before they can find a cure.

LEWIS GOES FOR GOLD

August 31, Los Angeles Star of the main Olympic Games was American athlete Carl Lewis. He won three gold medals for sprinting, and set an Olympic record for the 200 m. Lewis also won a gold medal in the long jump, giving him a total of four.

RONALD REAGAN REELECTED

Nov. 6, Washington President Reagan has been reelected to another four-year term of office. He beat Democrat Walter Mondale by a huge majority. Six out of every ten American citizens voted for Reagan.

Reagan is one of the most popular presidents of this century. The former film star is known as the "Great Communicator." A great many Americans particularly admire his tough, straightforward speeches on foreign policy.

CHEMICAL DISASTER AT BHOPAL

Dec. 10, Bhopal, India A leak at a chemical factory has killed at least 2,500 people, and injured as many as 250,000. A cloud of poisonous gas escaped from the factory. It spread over the surrounding area, where thousands of people live. Many of the injured have been blinded.

Local people are angry with the American owners. They say that not enough attention was paid to safety precautions in the factory.

THRILLING THE WORLD

Dec. 31, Los Angeles Pop star of the year is 26-year-old Michael Jackson. Born in Gary, Indiana, in 1958, as a child he sang and danced with his brothers in a group called the Jackson Five. Jackson now has a hugely successful solo career. His album *Thriller* has become a record-breaking best-seller around the world.

BHOPAL VICTIM DESCRIBES DISASTER

Dec. 6, India "We were choking and our eyes were burning. We could barely see the road through the fog, and sirens were blaring. We didn't know which way to run. Everybody was very confused. Mothers didn't know their children had died, children didn't know their mothers had died, and men didn't know their whole families had died."

(Ahmed Khan, quoted in *The Times*)

1985

GORBACHEV COMES TO POWER

March 11, Moscow Mikhail Gorbachev is the new leader of Russia. He replaces the elderly Konstantin Chernenko who was in power for only 13 months. Chernenko took over when Andropov died last year. At 56, Gorbachev is the youngest member of the Russian leadership, and he is expected to be in favor of economic reform.

The Russian economy is extremely inefficient, and there are always shortages of basic supplies in the shops. Gorbachev will want factories to produce more consumer goods, and fewer military products. This could make him unpopular with Russian military chiefs.

SOCCER RIOT KILLS 41 FANS

May 29, Brussels, Belgium Violent English soccer fans have been blamed for the deaths of 41 Italian and Belgian spectators at the Heysel stadium. The trouble started before the European Cup Final between teams from England and Italy. A crowd of English supporters charged at a group of Italian fans, causing a stampede. Most of the dead were crushed by a wall that collapsed under the weight of bodies; others were trampled to death. A group of English fans has been detained.

English soccer fans have a reputation for violence and drunkenness. This latest incident is likely to result in English teams being banned from European competitions.

"LIVE AID" FOR ETHIOPIA

July 7, Philadelphia Thanks to linked worldwide television, one-third of the world's population watched two live pop concerts for charity today. Labeled "Live Aid," the concerts took place simultaneously, one here and one in London. Throughout the day, rock and pop celebrities asked viewers to give money for famine relief in Ethiopia. About $53 million was raised. The concerts were the idea of Bob Geldof, Irish fund-raiser and rock singer. He also recorded the huge hit record "Do They Know It's Christmas?" last year. The money from its sales also went to Ethiopia.

Bob Geldof asks fans to give money, at the Live Aid concert in London.

EARTHQUAKE IN MEXICO

Sept. 20, Mexico City A devastating earthquake hit the world's largest city yesterday. More than 2,000 people are reported killed, and thousands more have been injured. Many lie trapped beneath piles of rubble. The earthquake struck near the center of the city, and dozens of multistoried buildings have collapsed. Mexican rescue squads are working night and day looking for survivors. Several foreign governments have sent help.

PLO HIJACKS CRUISE SHIP

Oct. 7, Rome, Italy Gunmen of the Palestine Liberation Organization have seized the *Achille Lauro* an Italian cruise ship. They are holding 450 passengers hostage. One American passenger has already been killed. The hijackers are demanding the release of Palestinian prisoners from Israeli jails. However, the Israeli government is very unlikely to give in to their demands.

ITALY LETS HIJACKERS GO FREE

Oct. 17, Rome, Italy After a bizarre sequence of events, the PLO hijackers have been allowed to go free. The gunmen surrendered in return for an aircraft that would take them to Tunisia. After taking off, they were forced down by American jet fighters and landed in Sicily. The Palestinians were arrested by the Italians, but then allowed to go free. The U.S. government protested strongly. The Italian government has resigned.

WRECK OF *TITANIC* FOUND

Sept. 3, Paris A joint French-American underwater team has found the wreck of the *Titanic*, about 13,000 feet (4,000 meters) below the surface of the Atlantic Ocean. The *Titanic* was hailed as "unsinkable" when it was launched in 1912. But on the very first voyage, it hit an iceberg and sank, with the loss of over 1,500 lives. Scientists from the team say that most of the huge ship is lying in one piece on the seabed.

ANGLO-IRISH AGREEMENT SIGNED

Nov. 15, Belfast, Northern Ireland The British and Irish governments have signed a historic agreement. The government of the Irish Republic will be allowed a say in British policy toward the province of Northern Ireland. There will be closer cooperation between British and Irish security forces. Protestant politicians in Northern Ireland are strongly against the agreement.

Northern Irish attack the agreement.

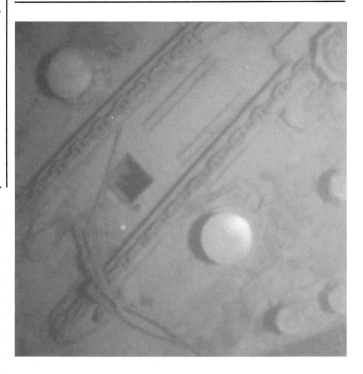

Anchor chains can be seen on the bow of the *Titanic,* thousands of feet down on the seabed.

NEWS IN BRIEF . . .

ROCK HUDSON DIES OF AIDS

Oct. 2, Hollywood Famous leading man Rock Hudson died today of AIDS. He was 59. Hudson had just recently admitted to having the disease, the first major star to do so. For the past year he has been losing weight and looking ill. Hudson appeared in films, such as *Magnificent Obsession, Giant,* and *Pillow Talk* and in the very popular television series *McMillan and Wife.*

AIDS EPIDEMIC DECLARED

Sept. 13, Geneva, Switzerland The World Health Organization has said that there is now a worldwide epidemic of AIDS. Many countries have education programs to fight the spread of the disease, and AIDS warnings appear on TV. Although we now understand how the virus is transmitted, there is no known cure for the disease.

FRENCH AGENTS JAILED

Nov. 21, Auckland, New Zealand Two French secret agents have been jailed for sinking the ship *Rainbow Warrior* and killing one of the crew. *Rainbow Warrior* belonged to the international environmental organization Greenpeace. The ship was sunk here four months ago by a bomb planted under the hull. *Rainbow Warrior* had often been used to protest and disrupt French nuclear weapons tests in the Pacific Ocean. The New Zealand authorities believe that the ship was sunk on the orders of the French government. One of the agents sent to prison today was a French Army diving instructor.

MIXED MARRIAGE IN SOUTH AFRICA

June 15, Pretoria South Africa's first mixed marriage, between people of different races, took place today. Two months ago, the government said that the ban on mixed marriages was over. Despite such changes in the laws that uphold the apartheid regime, a two-tier system is still in force here. People of color are not full citizens because they are not allowed to vote.

CONTRACEPTIVES LEGALIZED IN IRELAND

Feb. 20, Dublin, Ireland The Dail, the Irish parliament, has voted to allow contraceptives to be sold in shops. Ireland is strongly influenced by the Catholic Church, which does not condone artificial contraception. Previously, Irish people could only obtain contraceptives from doctors. Now they will be able to buy them in supermarkets and shops, as in other countries.

ORSON WELLES DIES

Oct. 10, Hollywood Orson Welles, the brilliant but erratic American filmmaker, has died at the age of 70. Orson Welles will be best remembered for *Citizen Kane,* which is considered by many to be the finest film ever made. Welles both directed the film and appeared in the leading role.

CRACK HITS NYC STREETS

Nov. 29, New York Crack, a new form of cocaine, has hit New York City. Crack is smoked rather than being inhaled like powdered cocaine. It is less expensive and almost immediately addictive. It is purified from powdered cocaine into crystals and so is much more concentrated. Police fear huge numbers of new addicts and the crime that comes with them. Police have raided a number of crack "factories." But the drug seems to be spreading quickly, not only here, but in the suburbs and other cities.

1986

NUCLEAR DISASTER IN RUSSIA

CHERNOBYL REACTOR EXPLODES

May 1, Chernobyl, Russia A reactor at a Russian nuclear power station has exploded and caught fire. Troops and emergency services are making desperate efforts to put out the flames. The task is extremely dangerous because of radioactivity from the damaged reactor. Some of the firefighters are certain to die from radiation poisoning.

The explosion happened five days ago at Chernobyl in southern Russia. It is the most serious nuclear accident ever known. Thousands of local people have been evacuated, because of the dangers of radiation. Experts say that radioactivity from Chernobyl will drift across Western Europe, contaminating food supplies.

A helicopter sprays decontaminates at the Chernobyl nuclear power plant.

CONTAMINATION SPREADS ACROSS EUROPE

June 20, New York The British government reported today that sheep from parts of northern England have been contaminated with radiation from Chernobyl. The government has banned the selling of these sheep for food. Other European governments have had to take similar action. In Poland, authorities have banned the sale of milk from certain areas. Some storekeepers have been using Geiger counters to prove that their goods are uncontaminated.

SPACE SHUTTLE EXPLODES

Jan. 28, Cape Kennedy The space shuttle *Challenger* exploded 70 seconds after it was launched this morning. The shuttle was engulfed in a ball of flame, and all seven astronauts on board were killed. One of them, Sharon Christa McAuliffe, was the first private American citizen to be sent into space. She was a schoolteacher.

The *Challenger* accident is the most serious setback ever suffered by the U.S. space program. All further shuttle flights have been postponed until scientists have discovered the exact cause of the disaster.

MARCOS FLEES PHILIPPINES

Feb. 25, Manila, Philippines President Ferdinand Marcos has been toppled from power by the widow of an assassinated politician. The new leader of the Philippines is Mrs. Corazon Aquino.

Earlier this month, Marcos rigged the elections in which Mrs. Aquino was a candidate, and declared himself the winner. This afternoon, crowds of Aquino supporters stormed Marcos's palace. He and his wife escaped by helicopter under cover of darkness, leaving Mrs. Aquino in charge of the country. During his 20 years in power, Marcos is believed to have stolen millions of dollars from the national treasury.

Mrs. Corazon Aquino with her delighted supporters.

SWEDISH PRIME MINISTER ASSASSINATED

Feb. 28, Stockholm, Sweden Olaf Palme, the Swedish prime minister, was shot dead tonight. The assassin escaped on foot, and the Swedish police have launched a widespread search for the killer. Mr. Palme was walking home from a movie theater when the attack took place.

U.S. PLANES BOMB LIBYA

April 15, Tripoli, Libya American bombers have carried out a series of air attacks against what are believed to be terrorist targets here. Libya's President Muammar Qaddafi escaped when bombs fell near his palace, but his daughter was killed.

The attacks were in retaliation for Libya's involvement in the recent terrorist bombing of U.S. servicemen in Germany.

"IRANGATE" SCANDAL BREAKS

Nov. 30, Washington A political scandal threatens the career of President Reagan. The President and his advisors are accused of making secret arms deals with Iran, against U.S. policy. In return for arms, the Iranians helped release U.S. hostages held in Lebanon. Money from the deals was sent to right-wing Contra rebels in Nicaragua. This new scandal has been dubbed "Irangate" by the press.

A PARTY FOR "MISS LIBERTY"

Oct. 28, New York A formal ceremony and grand celebration was held today, exactly 100 years after the original dedication of the Statue of Liberty. After having been closed for major repairs, the great symbol of hope reopened to visitors on last July 4 as part of the Independence Day celebrations. The statue was a gift from the French people, and President Reagan lunched with President François Mitterrand of France on July 4.

NEWS IN BRIEF . . .

HALLEY'S COMET INVESTIGATED

March 6, Moscow The Soviet spacecraft *Vega 1* flew within 5,500 miles (8,800 km) of Halley's Comet today. Scientists from the U.S. and many other countries were invited to watch this close encounter. *Vega 1* sent back pictures when it reached its closest point. Other spacecraft from the U.S., Japan, and the European Space Agency have also come close to the comet. They confirm that it is made up mainly of ice, gas, and dust. Astronomers have waited eagerly to see the comet, which appears every 76 years.

ANOTHER ACTOR IN POLITICS

April 8, Calif. Another American film actor has gone into politics. Clint Eastwood has been elected mayor of Carmel-by-the-Sea, a California tourist resort. Eastwood rose to stardom in westerns made in Europe during the 1960s. Later, he played the gun-happy detective in *Dirty Harry* and its sequels. The job of the mayor is only part-time, however. Eastwood will continue to make movies, both as actor and director.

HENRY MOORE DIES

Aug. 31, London British sculptor Henry Moore died today. Moore is famous for his massive, curving stone shapes pierced by holes. During World War II, he made many drawings of people sheltering down in the London Underground from air raids, and these influenced his later work. Many of his sculptures are not in art galleries. They are sited in open spaces in cities and in the countryside.

CHEMICALS POLLUTE RHINE

Nov. 10, Basel, Switzerland A fire in a chemical warehouse here has caused a major environmental disaster. More than 1,000 tons of extremely poisonous chemicals were released into the waters of the Rhine. Fish are dying, and experts say the river itself could actually "die." Four European countries have stopped using Rhine water for drinking.

FLYING AROUND THE WORLD

Dec. 12, Calif. Two Americans, one the daughter of a test pilot, have just completed the first nonstop flight around the world without refueling. Their oddly-shaped *Voyager* aircraft flew for nine days on a single load of fuel. With its huge wingspan, it operates like a glider. During their long flight, pilots Richard Rutan and Jeana Yeager took turns sleeping.

Voyager took off on its around-the-world flight with its hollow, carbon fiber wings full of fuel.

1987

REFORMS ANNOUNCED IN RUSSIA

Jan. 29, Moscow President Mikhail Gorbachev has called for greater democracy in Russian politics. He said that central control and lack of choice were to blame for the stagnation of the Russian economy. In the future, Gorbachev wants voters to have a choice of candidates in local elections. During his speech, the Russian president used two key words to summarize his proposed reforms: *glasnost* and *perestroika*.

Glasnost means openness. If Russia is to develop, the authorities must allow greater freedom of information and criticism. At present, all state information is secret. Open criticism of the government can land citizens in jail. In the past, dissidents have even been confined in mental hospitals.

Perestroika means reconstruction. This refers to the task of transforming the Russian economy and political system. Factories need to be reequipped with modern machinery, and the people must be

Gorbachev on a recent visit to Prague.

given a greater say in deciding government policy.

President Gorbachev will need to be very cautious in making these changes. Many of the older members of the Communist party are bitterly opposed to any type of reform. They believe that any relaxation of control will bring about a total collapse of the Communist system in Russia.

IRANIAN PILGRIMS GO ON RAMPAGE

July 30, Mecca, Saudi Arabia Iranian pilgrims visiting Mecca were involved in serious rioting today. The Saudi Arabian police opened fire on the rioters, and more than 100 are believed to have been killed during the violence.

The hajj, or pilgrimage to Mecca, is an annual event open to Muslims from all over the world. Muslims try to make the hajj at least once in a lifetime. The riots began when thousands of Iranian fundamentalists used the hajj for demonstrations against America and Israel.

MUJAHADDIN CONTINUE STRUGGLE

Sept. 30, Kandahar, Afghanistan Twenty mujahaddin (freedom fighters) gathered in the shadows around a Russian army post during a recent attack. Some of them carried captured Russian weapons. Others had guns bought with money sent from rich Muslim countries such as Saudi Arabia. At a signal, they fired rockets and machine guns at the Russians, then vanished into the night.

After nearly seven years of military occupation, the Russians are still no nearer to subduing the mujahaddin, despite their helicopters and tanks.

HEAVY FIGHTING IN SRI LANKA

Oct. 11, Jafna, Sri Lanka Indian troops are engaged in heavy fighting against Tamil Tiger guerrillas. Indian tanks are being used in house-to-house fighting in the Tamil stronghold of Jafna. The Indians came to Sri Lanka to enforce a cease-fire between the Tamils and government forces, and they are now trying to disarm the Tigers.

The Tamil Tigers want a separate Tamil state. For several years they have been using terror tactics against the Sri Lankan government. Open warfare broke out earlier this year. Thousands of people, many of them civilians, have been killed.

WORLDWIDE STOCK MARKET CRASH

Oct. 19, New York, London, Tokyo Stock markets around the world have tumbled today. It is already being called "Black Monday." The trouble began on Friday with the panic selling of shares in New York. After the weekend, the selling continued and spread to other financial centers. In New York, stocks lost more than 20 percent of their value today. In London, prices fell by 10 percent.

Experts are blaming the size of the crash on computerized dealing systems. Once the market dropped, the computers were programmed to sell everything. The crash follows five years of rising markets, and many people had become used to the idea that stocks were an easy way to make money. Millions of investors around the world have suddenly become poorer. Some financial companies are certain to go out of business.

FIJI GOES INDEPENDENT

Oct. 15, Nadi, Fiji Fiji is to become an independent republic, Colonel Sitiveni Rabuka announced today. Rabuka has been Fiji's leader since he seized power in May. His coup was supported by most of the native Fijians, who felt threatened by the island's Indian population. Half the people living in Fiji are Indians, but they had nearly all the seats in Fiji's parliament. Colonel Rabuka says he will give power back to the native population.

NUCLEAR ARMS REDUCTION TREATY

Dec. 8, Washington President Reagan and President Gorbachev have signed the first treaty that will reduce the number of nuclear missiles. Both superpowers will dismantle their short- and medium-range missiles. This includes the cruise missiles kept in Britain and other European countries. These moves towards nuclear arms reduction have been welcomed throughout the world. It seems the cold war is nearly over.

NEWS IN BRIEF . . .

ANDY WARHOL DIES

Feb. 22, New York The most famous exponent of Pop Art died in a hospital tonight. During the Sixties and Seventies, Warhol was among the most influential artists in the world. He will be best remembered for his paintings of soup cans, and his images of Marilyn Monroe. But Warhol was more than just a painter and filmmaker. He was a philosopher of this age of the mass media. He said that in the future, television would make everybody famous for 15 minutes.

MILLIONS FOR A VAN GOGH

March 30, London A painting of a bowl of flowers has been sold to a Japanese insurance company for over $32 million. *Sunflowers* by Vincent Van Gogh is one of the world's most famous paintings, and it has been reproduced thousands of times. When the original was auctioned off today, it set a world record price of $32,670,000.

GERMAN TEENAGER LANDS IN RED SQUARE

May 28, Moscow A 19-year-old German boy has flown a light aircraft through Russian air defenses and landed it next to the Kremlin in Moscow. Mathias Rust took off from Helsinki, Finland, and flew all the way to the Russian capital. After he landed, Rust signed autographs for passersby before being arrested by Russian police.

TORNADO HITS TEXAS

May 24, Pecos, Texas A killer tornado struck the small town of Saragosa in Reeves County two days ago. This sparsely populated area of western Texas was the scene of a violent, twisting windstorm that left 29 people dead. The number of injured and the amount of damage is not yet known.

1988

RUSSIAN OCCUPATION OF AFGHANISTAN ENDS

May 15, Kabul, Afghanistan The first convoy of Russian soldiers left for home today. A peace treaty was signed last month in Geneva between four nations: Afghanistan, Pakistan, Russia, and the U.S. The treaty ends the nine-year Russian occupation of Afghanistan. All Russian troops must be out of the country by the end of this year.

Although there is now a cease-fire, the Russians can expect to be attacked by mujahaddin all the way to the border. When the Russians have all gone, the mujahaddin's enemy will be the government troops that defend the main towns. Few people expect the government to survive.

At present there are about 100,000 Russian soldiers and airmen in Afghanistan. There are an unknown number of secret police. During the last nine years, some 13,000 Russian servicemen have been killed on active service here, and a further 35,000 have been wounded.

Mujahaddin carry on the fight in Afghanistan.

U.S. SHIP SHOOTS DOWN IRANIAN AIRLINER

July 3, Persian Gulf In a tragic misunderstanding, a United States ship the *Vincennes* has shot down an Iranian civil airliner. All 290 people on board the airliner were killed.

The *Vincennes* was engaged on a routine patrol of the Persian Gulf to protect neutral shipping from attack by Iranian "Silkworm" missiles. At the time of the incident, the U.S. ship was involved in a small sea battle with Iranian patrol boats. Radar operators aboard the *Vincennes* mistook the airliner for an attacking jet fighter in the heat of the battle. An antiaircraft missile scored a direct hit.

Our government has apologized for the incident, and sent messages of sympathy to the relatives of those killed. Even though it was an accident, the loss of the airliner is sure to stir up anti-American feeling in Iran.

IRAN AND IRAQ STOP FIGHTING

July 20, Geneva, Switzerland Both sides in the war between Iran and Iraq have agreed to a cease-fire arranged by the United Nations. This war has cost hundreds of thousands of lives, and has left both countries devastated. The war has been little reported, and most of the fighting has taken place on barren mountains and in deserts. Earlier this year, during the "war of the cities," civilians were killed during bombardment by long-range missiles. Last year, Iraq used mustard gas and nerve gas to stop Iranian attacks. Earlier, they used poison gas to kill those sympathetic to Iran inside Iraq. The other side is no better. The Iranians have sent children as young as 13 to the front line.

BUSH IS ELECTED PRESIDENT

Nov. 8, Washington Republican George Bush, Ronald Reagan's Vice-President, has been elected President of the United States. Bush beat the Democratic contender, Michael Dukakis of Massachusetts, by a significant majority. Dan Quayle is to be the new Vice-President. However, Bush is not as popular as Reagan has been. Less than half those Americans eligible to vote actually went to the polls, making this the lowest turnout since 1924.

PAKISTAN HAS WOMAN PREMIER

Dec. 2, Islamabad, Pakistan Following this month's elections, Benazir Bhutto was today sworn in as Pakistan's first woman prime minister. She is the first woman leader of a Muslim country. Ms. Bhutto is the daughter of former president Ali Bhutto, who was overthrown and then executed by President Zia in the 1970s. She takes over from a caretaker government that was installed after President Zia was assassinated in August.

Vice-President Bush addresses flag-waving supporters during a campaign visit on September 29.

PALESTINIANS RECOGNIZE ISRAEL

Dec. 13, Geneva, Switzerland At the General Assembly of the UN, Yasser Arafat has said that the Palestinians recognize the existence of Israel and renounce terrorism. The General Assembly had to meet in Geneva, because the Americans would not give Arafat a visa to visit New York.

The Palestinian *intifada*, or uprising, in the Israeli-occupied territories is now entering its second year. Arab-owned shops and businesses remain closed. The refugee camps are under strict curfew. Gangs of Palestinian youths continue to taunt Israeli soldiers. So far, 300 Palestinians have been shot dead, and 100 have died of beatings and from exposure to tear gas.

U.S. AIRLINER BLOWN UP IN MIDAIR

Dec. 21, Frankfurt, W. Germany A Pan Am Boeing 747 exploded and crashed on its way to the U.S. today. All 259 people on board were killed, and wreckage was strewn over a wide area. The flight from Frankfurt to New York was packed with people going home for Christmas when the plane exploded in midair. A large piece of wreckage fell on the Scottish town of Lockerbie, killing 11 people. An Iranian terrorist bombing is suspected.

CUBAN TROOPS TO QUIT AFRICA

Dec. 22, Geneva, Switzerland Representatives from Angola, Cuba, and South Africa today signed an agreement that will lead to the independence of Namibia. Under the agreement, Cuban troops will leave Angola. In return, South African troops will leave Namibia.

There are about 50,000 Cuban troops in Angola. Some have been there for more than ten years. Under the agreement, they must go by July 1991.

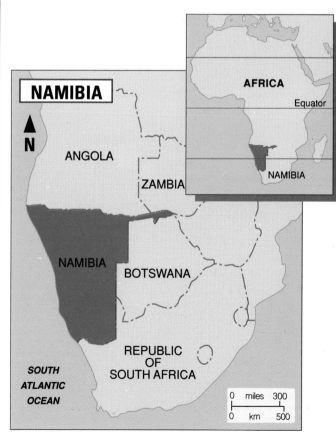

NEWS IN BRIEF . . .

NEW YEAR SUPERPOWER GOODWILL

Jan. 1, Washington and Moscow The USSR and America were linked by television at the start of the year. For the first time, Russian television showed a five-minute New Year's Day speech from President Reagan. In return, our government arranged for the American TV companies to show a similar speech by President Gorbachev. Both the speeches contained messages of goodwill and hope for the future.

AUSTRALIAN BICENTENNIAL

Jan. 26, Sydney, Australia Australia celebrates being 200 years old today. During the festivities a fleet of tall ships is anchoring in Sydney Harbor. Sailing ships from all over the world have gathered here to help the nation celebrate.

Not everybody is having a party. A few of the country's Aborigines are using the bicentennial as a platform for protest. They want a much greater say in the development of what was once their land.

RUSSIAN CHRISTIANS CELEBRATE

June 5, Moscow Today the Soviet people celebrated one thousand years of Christianity in their country. The Eastern Orthodox Church was banned throughout the reign of Lenin, Stalin, and subsequent hard-line leaders. They imposed atheism on the people as part of the Communist system. However, most people kept their faith alive in secret.

DRUG BARON SENTENCED

May 19, Jacksonville, Florida A Colombian drug baron Carlos Lehder was today sentenced to life imprisonment plus 150 years. He had smuggled three tons of cocaine into the United States. He was one of the leaders of the Medellin cartel, a drug ring that smuggles much of the cocaine that enters America. He was arrested by the Colombian authorities and sent here for trial.

U.S. government anti-drug policy does much more than just give stiff prison sentences to smugglers. During recent months, our troops have been in Bolivia, finding and destroying jungle drug factories.

EARTHQUAKE IN ARMENIA

Dec. 7, Armenia, southern Russia A massive earthquake has struck the district of Armenia. It is estimated that over 55,000 people have been killed. Nearly half a million have been made homeless in temperatures below freezing. Gorbachev has cut short an overseas visit in order to take charge of the relief operation. Several foreign governments have offered to

NORTH SEA GAS RIG EXPLODES

July 7, Scotland An offshore gas platform Piper Alpha has exploded and caught fire. At least 160 workers have been killed and dozens more injured; 64 were rescued. Emergency services have been fighting the flames through the night, and helicopters are still searching for survivors. It seems the disaster was caused by the failure of a safety valve, which allowed the buildup of flammable gas.

send food, medical teams, and rescue equipment. However, rescue work is difficult because the Armenian countryside is isolated and mountainous.

1989

MASSACRE IN TIAN-AN-MEN SQUARE

June 4, Beijing, China The Chinese authorities have crushed the democracy movement, which was led by students. Between two and five thousand people have been killed during two days of savage repression. Thousands more have been seriously injured. The worst of the violence occurred when soldiers and tanks moved into Tian-an-men Square in the center of Beijing early this morning. Students' leaders and crowds of their supporters had gathered in the square as a final protest. Many were shot as the soldiers fired at random into the crowds. Others were crushed beneath tanks.

During the last few weeks, it appeared that the movement for democracy was being accepted by China's Communist leadership. However, all hopes of reform have now been wiped out. Deng Xiaoping, China's elderly leader, praised the army for its action against the threat of "counter-revolutionary agitators."

CITIZENS KILLED IN SOVIET GEORGIA

April 9, Georgia, USSR Russian internal security troops killed 16 civilian demonstrators early this morning. More than 200 were hurt. This is the worst example of state brutality for many years. The incident happened during a demonstration in Tbilisi, the capital of the Republic of Georgia.

Earlier, up to 100,000 Georgians had filled the streets, calling for Georgia to become independent. The security troops moved in on a crowd of demonstrators that had surrounded the town hall. Most of those killed were women; some were clubbed to death, others were sprayed with poison gas, which choked and suffocated them.

Georgia is one of the largest of the 16 republics that make up the USSR. As in most other republics, the native people form a separate ethnic group. Unrest from its ethnic peoples is one of the biggest problems currently facing Russia's leadership. Ethnic unrest could cause Russia to break apart into a number of smaller nations.

HUNGARY OPENS BORDER

Sept. 12, Budapest, Hungary The Hungarian government has relaxed controls over its border with Austria. As a result, thousands of East Germans are crossing over to Western Europe. All summer, East Germans have been gathering in Hungary, hoping to escape. Many have been camping out in the grounds of foreign embassies rather than return home. Hungary's Communist neighbors have loudly criticized the government's action. They say Hungary is encouraging the move to democracy in other countries.

SOLIDARITY WINS POLISH ELECTIONS

June 4, Warsaw, Poland Solidarity has won all but one of the available seats in the Polish elections. The organization that started out as a trade union has become the country's ruling political party. Poland is the first country in Eastern Europe to elect a non-Communist government. Until April, Solidarity was an illegal organization.

Supporters applaud the news that Solidarity is no longer an illegal organization.

MASSIVE PRO-DEMOCRACY DEMONSTRATION

Nov. 4, East Berlin More than 500,000 East Berliners crowded into the city streets tonight. They heard speeches by opponents of the Communist government. This is the largest pro-democracy demonstration so far, and its size is a sign that the government is beginning to lose control. As well as calling for the Berlin Wall to be pulled down, the crowds also shouted for East and West Germany to be reunited.

BERLIN WALL OPENED

Nov. 10, East Berlin, Germany East German border guards tonight opened the gates and checkpoints in the Berlin Wall. For the first time in 28 years, Berliners can now pass through freely.

This is the most surprising event so far in a wave of democracy that appears to be sweeping across Eastern Europe. Throughout this summer, Communist governments have been increasingly attacked by the people. There have been massive pro-democracy demonstrations. It looks as though the Iron Curtain is finally being lifted.

GERMANS FREE TO CROSS BERLIN WALL

Nov. 10, Berlin "I have stamped other people's passports for four years, and I never thought I would stand on the other side of the counter, I can't believe it." —a border guard.

"When I heard the news I didn't think about a visa, I just got into my car and drove to the border. It was like a dream." —young East German.

"We just wanted to put a foot over the line; we were like children, we just couldn't wait. Our little boy is at home asleep, so we have to go straight back." —East German couple.

"It is breathtaking. All those years I learnt about the anti-fascist protection barrier—it is as if our country has finally opened its eyes to reality." —a history student.

(All quoted in *The Times*)

DEMOCRATIC PRESIDENT FOR CZECHOSLOVAKIA

Dec. 29, Prague, Czechoslovakia The playwright Vaclav Havel has been elected the new president of Czechoslovakia. He was the unanimous choice of the country's new Popular Assembly. Havel is Czechoslovakia's first non-Communist head of state since 1948.

The Popular Assembly has also appointed Alexander Dubček as its first chairman. Dubček tried to liberalize Czech politics in 1968. His efforts were crushed by a Russian invasion. Although Communists still have many top jobs, their power is rapidly declining. The new focus of Czech politics is "Civic Forum," an alliance of the old opposition groups.

ANC LEADER RELEASED

Oct. 15, Pretoria, South Africa The winds of change are blowing in South Africa. Today, the government released eight political prisoners, including Walter Sisulu, a leading member of the African National Congress (ANC). Sisulu has been imprisoned since 1964, when he was jailed with Nelson Mandela. Announcing the release, President De Klerk stated that the ANC would remain a banned organization. De Klerk did not say whether Mandela will also be released.

REVOLUTION IN ROMANIA

Dec. 25, Sofia, Romania After three days of bitter street fighting, Romania's Communist government has been overthrown. Its hated dictator, President Nicolai Ceausescu, is dead. An alliance of soldiers and citizens has defeated the Securitate, the secret police who remained loyal to the president.

Weeks of unrest broke into open revolution on December 22, when crowds began booing a speech by the president. Within minutes, the crowd's mood had turned ugly. Ceausescu escaped from the presidential palace by helicopter. He was soon captured, and after a court-martial, he and his wife were executed by firing squad. Tonight, the streets of Sofia still ring with gunfire, as police and the army hunt the last few Securitate men.

President Nicolai Ceausescu and his wife, Elena, are shown on television during their trial.

NEWS IN BRIEF . . .

OIL SPILL IN ALASKA

March 25, Anchorage The *Exxon Valdez* is an Exxon Corporation oil tanker. Yesterday, loaded with crude oil from the Trans Alaska Pipeline, it ran aground on an undersea reef and broke open. A huge amount of oil was spilled into Prince William Sound, a beautiful, unspoiled area. The oil slick now covers about an eight-mile-long, three-mile-wide stretch of water. Environmentalists say the effects of this disaster, particularly on wildlife, may last for years.

AUTHOR IN HIDING

Feb. 14, London British author Salman Rushdie has gone into hiding after threats on his life. These threats followed upon the publication of his new book *The Satanic Verses*. Islamic scholars claim that the book is deeply insulting to all Muslims. In Tehran, the Ayatollah Khomeini has condemned Rushdie, and has asked all Muslims to try to kill him. The British government has protested to Iran.

FLAG BURNING LEGAL

June 21, Washington In a 5 to 4 vote, the Supreme Court decided that burning the U.S. flag as a form of political protest is constitutional. It is protected by the First Amendment, which guarantees citizens the right to free speech. This decision is causing fierce debate. Free speech defenders claim it as a victory. Others are calling for a new amendment to protect the flag.

SAN FRANCISCO EARTHQUAKE

Oct. 18, San Francisco A powerful earthquake shook this California city today. More than 250 people were killed, and hundreds more were injured. The 15-second quake brought down a stretch of elevated highway. Many of the dead and injured were trapped in their cars when the earthquake struck. The city lies on a geological fault.

A businessman walks to work through rubble in San Francisco.

SINGLE CURRENCY FOR EUROPE

Dec. 30, Brussels, Belgium The European Economic Community has agreed in principle to an economic and monetary union. This means that all member nations will one day use the same money. Some countries, such as Britain, are not happy with the decision. They see monetary union as the first step towards a single European state. Their sense of national identity rejects the idea of a unified Europe. Those who support it say it would help trade.

U.S. INVADES PANAMA

Dec. 20, Panama City In a military action called "Operation Just Cause," ordered by President Bush, 24,000 U.S. troops have invaded Panama. The action follows a series of anti-American incidents. The most serious of these was the killing of a U.S. marine by Panamanian soldiers. However, the main purpose of the invasion is to capture General Manuel Noriega, virtual dictator of Panama. He is wanted in the United States on drug trafficking charges.

PEOPLE OF THE EIGHTIES

Ronald Reagan 1911–

After a successful career as a film actor, Reagan turned to politics. During 1967–1975 he served as governor of California. He was elected President in 1980; people liked his tough, rather old-fashioned views. Under his leadership, military spending increased, and foreign policy was more aggressive. During his second four-year term in office, Reagan was involved in the "Irangate" scandal. He retired in 1988.

Margaret Thatcher 1925–

Margaret Thatcher served as a minister in the British Conservative party government before being elected party leader in 1975. After she became prime minister in 1979, Mrs. Thatcher's tough financial policies soon brought inflation under control and revived the economy. In world affairs she earned international respect.

Under Margaret Thatcher's leadership many people became richer, but a new "underclass" of poor people also grew.

Ayatollah Ruhollah Khomeini 1900–1989

Iranian religious and political leader. Khomeini was trained as an Islamic scholar, and exiled from Iran by the Shah in 1964. In 1979, he returned to Iran to lead the Islamic revolution. Under his rule, Iran returned to a repressive system of religious law. Women, for instance, were forbidden to uncover their heads in public. In foreign policy, Khomeini was bitterly opposed both to the capitalist United States, and to atheist Russia.

Nelson Mandela 1918–

Black South African leader. Mandela has been a member of the African National Congress (ANC) since 1943. He was a supporter of the idea of an armed struggle against the apartheid regime of South Africa. In 1964, Mandela was arrested, tried for treason, and sentenced to life imprisonment. At various times during the 1970s and 1980s, people around the world campaigned for his release. The South African authorities refused to consider giving Mandela his freedom until he renounced the use of violence. He was freed in 1990, and was made leader of the ANC.

Sally Ride 1951–

American astronaut. In June 1983, Sally Ride, on the space shuttle *Challenger*, became the first American woman to travel in space. There she conducted important experiments on pharmaceutical production and the use of a "remote manipulator arm." Ride, with a Ph.D. in physics, became an astronaut candidate in 1978. In 1986, she officially investigated the tragic explosion of the *Challenger*. She left the astronaut program in 1987 to join the Stanford University Center for International Security and Arms Control.

Lech Walesa 1943–

Polish political leader. Walesa first became involved in politics during a shipyard strike in 1980. His unofficial movement grew into the Solidarity trade union. In 1983, Walesa was awarded the Nobel Peace Prize for the nonviolence of his campaign. In 1989 he was elected as a non-Communist member of the Polish parliament, and as president in 1990.

Mikhail Gorbachev 1931–

Russian leader. Gorbachev became a member of the Russian Politburo in 1980, and in 1985 he succeeded Chernenko as general secretary. Gorbachev has tried to reform Russia with his new ideas of *glasnost* (openness), and *perestroika* (reconstruction). He tried to tackle Russia's severe economic problems. Gorbachev has also faced the problems of ethnic and nationalist unrest inside Russia. During his leadership, Communist rule collapsed in Eastern Europe.

Yasser Arafat 1929–

Palestinian leader. Arafat first became involved in Palestinian politics in 1954, when he cofounded the Al Fatah guerrilla group. In 1969, he became chairman of the Palestine Liberation Organization (PLO). Since 1973, he has gradually reduced military action against Israel, and has emphasized diplomacy instead. In 1988, Arafat renounced terrorism, and stated that the PLO recognized the existence of Israel.

American Firsts

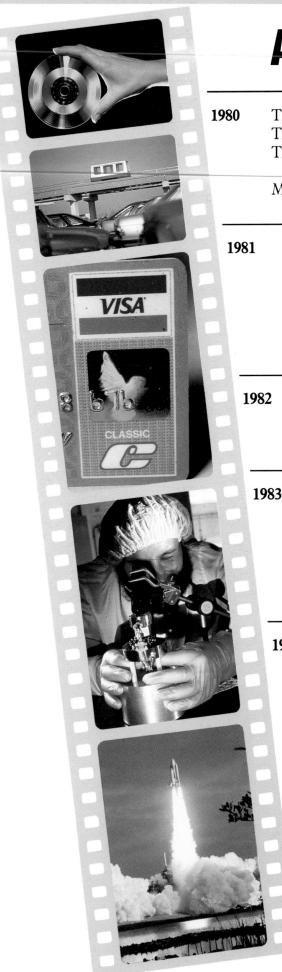

1980   The first women graduated from West Point.
The first solar-cell power plant was dedicated.
The first long-distance solar-powered airplane
flight was completed, Marana, Ariz.
Mary Decker was the first woman to run the mile
in less than 4.5 minutes, Philadelphia.

1981   *Voyager 2* found an area in the clouds
surrounding Saturn that is 300 times hotter
than the outer region of the sun.
I.B.M. launches its "personal" computer (P.C.).
Stephen Ptacek of the U.S. made the first
solar-powered flight across the English
Channel.

1982   The Food and Drug Administration approved
the first commercial product of genetic
engineering—insulin produced by bacteria.
Space shuttle *Columbia* flew its first mission.

1983   Apple Computer Company introduced the
"mouse" and pull-down "menus" to personal
computers.
The first artificially made chromosome was
created at Harvard University.
After 11 years in flight, *Pioneer X* became the
first spacecraft to leave the solar system.

1984   Scientists at the University of California,
Berkeley, cloned genes from an ancient
species.
Bruce McCandless and Robert Stewart of the
U.S. were the first to fly in space untethered to
a spacecraft.
NASA astronauts took photos of a planetary
system around the star Beta Pictoris.

1985   For the first time, lasers were used in the U.S. to
clean clogged arteries.
The atom smasher at Fermi National Accelerator
Laboratory, Batavia, Ill., produced energy
levels three times higher than any before.
Scientists at the University of California,
Berkeley, gained more evidence of a gigantic
black hole in the middle of our galaxy.

1986 The Food and Drug Administration approved the first vaccine for humans produced by genetic engineering.
Live Senate debates were broadcast for the first time.

1987 The last wild California condor was trapped and sent to a zoo for breeding.
David Gates, founder of Microsoft, is the microcomputer industry's first billionaire.

1988 Harvard scientists produced the first vertebrate (a mouse) to receive a U.S. patent.
U.S. surgeons implant the first plutonium-powered pacemaker to correct abnormal heart rhythms.
U.S. B-2 "Stealth" bomber was unveiled.

1989 Florida and Virginia allow DNA genetic "fingerprinting" as evidence in some rape cases.
Time, Inc. buys Warner Communications to create the world's largest entertainment group.

New words and expressions

The English language is always changing. New words are added to it, and old words are used in new ways. Here are a few of the words and expressions that first appeared or first came into popular use in the 1980s:

blue corn chips	Nimby
cross-training	point guard
dramedy	rocket scientist
fax	rock-jock
focus group	rust belt
fuzzball	shareware
gene therapy	sleezeball
home shopping	smoke and mirrors
hypertext	spin doctor
linear thinking	toxic waste
line item	wannabee
metal head	whole nine yards
moonwalk	wuss

How many of these words and expressions do we still use today? Do you know what they all mean?

Glossary

abdicate: to give up a throne.

apartheid: system of legalized racism in South Africa. Under apartheid, nonwhite people do not have the vote and are subject to a number of repressive and humiliating laws.

atheism: the belief that there is no God.

brainwashing: forcibly persuading someone to give up political, religious, or social beliefs and accept others in their place.

cartel: group of manufacturers who arrange to control the price of products.

cruise missile: small medium-range guided missile that can be very accurate. It can carry either a nuclear or conventional warhead.

fundamentalism: branch of religion that insists on the literal meaning of sacred texts.

Iron Curtain: name for the political and military border that existed between Western Europe and the Communist countries of Eastern Europe.

junta: group of people who control a government after seizing power.

militia: group of armed civilians. Some are well intentioned and well disciplined, others are little more than gangsters.

mujahaddin: Afghan Muslim guerrillas who fought against the Russian invaders and the Communist government of Afghanistan.

NATO: North Atlantic Treaty Organization; a military alliance that includes the United States and most of Western Europe.

Politburo: the inner cabinet that governed the former USSR and established policy.

public spending: money that a government spends in providing services for its citizens.

Shiite: belonging to a minority branch of the Muslim religion. Most Shiites live in Iran.

Star Wars: name for the system of satellite-mounted anti-missile defenses developed in the United States. Otherwise known as the Strategic Defense Initiative.

Further Reading

Anderson, Madelyn K. *Oil Spills.* Watts, 1990

Apartheid: Calibrations of Color, "Icarus World Issues Series." Rosen Publishing Group, 1991

Beshara, Raymond, et al. *What You Should Know About AIDS.* ERN, Inc., 1989

Burchard, S.H. *The Statue of Liberty: Birth to Rebirth.* Harcourt Brace Jovanovich, Inc., 1985

Carey, Helen and Greenberg, Judith. *How to Read a Newspaper.* Watts, 1983

——*How to Use Primary Sources.* Watts, 1983

Dudman, J. *Division of Berlin.* Rourke Corp.

Grey, Edward. *The Eighties,* "Decades" series. Raintree Steck-Vaughn, 1990

Husain, A. *Revolution in Iran.* Rourke Corp.

Lawson, Don. *America Held Hostage: From the Teheran Embassy Takeover to the Iran-Contra Affair.* Watts, 1991

Pfeiffer, Christine. *Poland: Land of Freedom Fighters.* Macmillan Child Group, 1991

Reische, Diana. *Arafat and the Palestine Liberation Organization.* Watts, 1991

Robbins, Neal E. *Ronald W. Reagan: Fortieth President of the United States.* Garrett Ed. Corp., 1990

Spangenberg, Ray and Moser, Diane. *Living and Working in Space.* Facts on File, 1989

Stefoff, Rebecca. *George H. Bush: Forty-First President of the United States.* Garrett Ed Corp., 1990

Teenage Soldiers Adult Wars, "Icarus World Issues." Rosen Publishing Group, 1991

Index

Afghanistan 31, 34
AIDS 14, 24, 27
Andropov, Yuri 17
Anglo-Irish agreement 26
Aquino, Corazon 29
Arafat, Yasser 16, 35, 43
Argentina 15, 16
Australia 21, 37

Belize 13
Berlin Wall 39
Bhopal 24
Bhutto, Benazir 35
Bush, George 9, 35

Carter, Jimmy 8, 9
Chernenko, Konstantin 25
Chernobyl 28
China 24, 38
cocaine 27, 37
corporal punishment 18
cruise missiles 14, 16
Czechoslovakia 40

Eastwood, Clint 30
Egypt 11
EPCOT (Disney World) 18
Ethiopia 23, 25

Falkland Islands 15, 16
Ferraro, Geraldine 22
Fiji 32
films 18, 27, 30

Gandhi, Indira 23
Geldof, Bob 25
Germany 10, 17, 39
Gorbachev, Mikhail 25, 31, 37, 43
Greenpeace 27
Grenada 20

Halley's Comet 30
hostages 8, 12

Hungary 38
Hussein, Saddam 9

IRA 23
Iran 8, 9, 12, 31, 34
"Irangate" 29
Iraq 9, 34
Ireland 26, 27
Israel 16, 35
Italy 26

Jackson, Michael 24
Jaruzelski, General Wojciech 12
Juan Carlos, king of Spain 12

Kenya 10
Khomeini, Ayatollah 8, 12, 20, 41, 42
Korea, South 19

Lebanon 16, 17, 20
Lennon, John 10
Lewis, Carl 24
Libya 29
Live Aid 25

Madonna 21
Mandela, Nelson 42
Marley, Bob 14
M.A.S.H. 21
Mexico 26
Mitterrand, François 13
"Moonies" (Sun Myung Moon) 18
Moore, Henry 30
Mugabe, Robert 9

Namibia 36
nuclear reactor 28
nuclear weapons 18, 32

O'Connor, Sandra Day 12
Olympic Games 10, 22
OPEC 21
Ortega, Daniel 16

Pakistan 35
Palestinians 35
Panama 41
Philippines 19, 29
PLO 16, 20, 26
Poland 9, 12, 13, 22, 39
Pope John Paul Ii 11
Popieluszko, Father Jerzy 22

Qaddafi, Colonel Muammar 29

Reagan, Ronald 9, 11, 12, 14, 20, 24, 29, 37, 42
Ride, Sally 43
Romania 22, 40

Sadat, Anwar 11
smallpox 10
Solidarity 9, 17, 22, 39
Sony "Walkman" 10
South Africa 27, 40
space shuttle 13, 28
Spain 12, 17
Sri Lanka 32
"Star Wars" defense 19
Statue of Liberty 29
Sweden 29
Syria 16, 20

Tamils 32
Thatcher, Margaret 15, 19, 42
Titanic 26

United States 12, 13, 14, 19, 20, 22, 29, 34, 36, 41
USSR 17, 31, 37, 38

Van Gogh, Vincent 33

Walesa, Lech 9, 21, 43
Welles, Orson 27

Zimbabwe 9